The Man in the High Castle

Philip K. Dick

A

SUMMARY, ANALYSIS & REVIEW

Note to Readers:

This is a Summary & Analysis of *The Man in the High Castle*, by Philip K. Dick. You are strongly encouraged to buy the full version.

TABLE OF CONTENTS

INTRODUCTION

One of the most prominent works of the writer's career and now a popular television series, Philip K. Dick's *The Man in the High Castle* is an award-winning, gripping tale of alternative history in the finest dystopian tradition. Tightly written and densely packed, it exemplifies why Dick is regarded as one of the greats not only of genre fiction, but of literature.

BOOK REVIEW

Philip K. Dick's classic work, *The Man in the High Castle*, depicts disparate events in an alternate history in which the Axis Powers won the Second World War and the United States has been largely partitioned between Japan and Germany. The novel follows several characters whose lives intersect only tangentially as they try to negotiate geopolitical tensions at the global and exceedingly local levels, working to move through a world still in turmoil even after fifteen years of dominion by ostensible allies, one that has peril for low and high alike.

There are always places where works falter, however. Dick has a long association with prophecy and madness, and there are parts of the novel that justify that association; the language is disjointed and difficult to follow. Too, the explication of Juliana's questioning of the I Ching seems somewhat heavy-handed, reading overly overtly as it questions in a seemingly adolescent fashion the nature of reality.

Even so, there are reasons *The Man in the High Castle* enjoys the classic status it does. It is a remarkably dense novel, following no fewer than four major plots and carrying heavy symbolic import as well as sustaining multiple discourses. It moves smoothly among the plotlines, and it manages most of its symbols and themes well, something particularly noteworthy given the relative brevity of the text; not many authors can pack as much into their work as Dick does and leave it readable. It is a work that reads well as an idle way to pass time, as well as one that rewards multiple readings and close attention, and it is therefore to be valued highly.

SETTING FOR THE STORY

The Man in the High Castle is set in an alternate 1962, one in which the Axis Powers won the Second World War and are consolidating their command not only of the world, but of other worlds entirely. Most of the text takes place in and around San Francisco, which operates under Japanese dominion, and Denver, which serves as a focal area of the parts of the United States that remain free of Axis governance. The world and the specific areas are familiar enough to Dick's initial readers and those that follow to be accessible, although its differences are chilling, indeed.

STORY PLOT ANALYSIS

Rather than reading as a single, monolithic story, the novel functions as a series of vignettes, roughly contemporaneous with one another, connected to one another only loosely. The focal narrative follows Frank Fink; his is connected to that of Juliana through their dissolved marriage, and it connects directly to that of Childan, which connects to that of Tagomi. Each proceeds forward in seeming tandem with the others, despite their relative lack of interaction with each other, speaking to the ease with which producers could take up the text as the basis for a television series. The progression works well as a series of individual vignettes that follows each plotline, making reading easy and allowing the many good things in the text to show forth.

MAIN & SECONDARY CHARACTER LIST

The novel follows four characters primarily. Frank "Frink" Fink serves as the unifying point of reference for the text (see "Analysis of a Key Character," below). His estranged wife, Juliana, occupies another plotline, as do Japanese trade official Nobosuke Tagomi and aspirant merchant Robert Childan. Other significant characters in the text include

- Betty Kasoura- prospective customer for Childan, Paul's wife
- Ed McCarthy- Frank's colleague
- Hawthorne Abdesnsen- author
- Hugo Reiss- German consul in San Francisco
- Joe Cinnadella- Swiss intelligence operative
- Paul Kasoura- prospective customer for Childan, Betty's husband
- Ramsey- Tagomi's aide
- Rudolf "Baynes" Wegener- German intelligence operative
- "Shinjiro Yatabe" Tedeki- Japanese general

BOOK OVERVIEW & STORY ANALYSIS

Below appears a summary of the text, with some analytical comments interspersed.

Chapter 1

Childan pours himself tea as he awaits an expected shipment and prepares his shop for the business of the day. He watches the crowds for a time before taking a call from Tagomi, who inquires about the shipment; it is to be a United States Civil War recruiting poster, for which Tagomi had left a large deposit. Childan reports failure to secure the item, and Tagomi upbraids him. Childan muses on the rebuke and its damage to his social status, and his thoughts turn to the world before the war. He arranges to take a representative sample of substitutes to Tagomi for review as other customers enter. Childan assesses the customers, the Kasouras, a married couple that expresses appreciation for his wares as Childan begins to lust after the woman. They discuss their reasons for being in San Francisco; the man is in the Japanese civil service. Childan discusses his wares with them, and they arrange a showing. As he Kasouras leave, Childan muses on the upcoming meeting with them, propriety and the meeting with Tagomi. He gathers materials and lights a marijuana cigarette.

Frank tries to roust himself, reviewing his situation. He had offended at work and is apt to be dismissed. Likely fallout from his doing so is rehearsed, as are the ways he can try to secure employment afterward. Relationships between the Rocky Mountain States – the remnants of the independent United States – and the Japanese-controlled Pacific states are noted. Thoughts of the South occur and are rejected due to the South's ongoing racism and Frank's Jewish identity. His personal history as a native New Yorker and former aspirant rebel is noted. An old landlord, his corruption and his disposition are noted, as well. The relative benignity of the Japanese government is noted, too. Frank listens to the news as he dresses, considering the differences between German advancement and Japanese consolidation. The horrors perpetrated by Germany on Africa are noted. Frank resolves to come to terms with his employer and consults the I Ching. It suggests humility in approaching the employer. He asks about his wife, too, considering her and the situation of the world; the oracle is not sanguine about the prospect of his rejoining Juliana, who is described in memory. Frank ponders who else in San Francisco consults the oracle and their results.

Chapter 2

Tagomi considers the I Ching in anticipation of the meeting with Childan. His office is described, and Tagomi considers his own client, as well as the imminently soured relationship therewith. The client's approach is described; German rocketry is involved, and Tagomi schools himself to disinterest against the arrival of the client, Baynes. Tagomi considers Baynes and summons a secretary to take dictation. They exchange pleasantries, and Tagomi begins giving dictation, logging his prognostication. He summons Ramsey for consultation about how to prepare their surroundings for Baynes. Tagomi resumes his logging, explicating the results of his oracular consultation. The industrial relationship between Japan and Germany is noted – and it is vastly in Germany's favor, given the distribution of resources across the world. The actual reason for Baynes's visit is hinted at, with Tagomi musing on the oddity of encryption that indicates Baynes is a spy.

Childan makes for Tagomi's office to attend his appointment with the trade officer. The racism still at work is noted as Childan settles in and muses on his upcoming presentation. The path and surroundings are described as

Childan continues to muse on etiquette and his ability to endure what he must. Ongoing slavery is noted, as is Childan's preoccupation with place and status. He muses favorably on German ethnic and racial policies. The horrors perpetrated in Africa are glossed, and Childan compares German "progress" with Japanese stasis. Childan arrives at Tagomi's offices, rehearsing how he came into dealing in American antiques and considering the identity of the client for whom he knows Tagomi is working to secure materials. Childan enters the office building uneasily and makes for Tagomi's office.

Chapter 3

Juliana watches a German rocket pass far overhead as the sun sets over the Rockies at the end of her workday. Her work as a judo instructor is noted as she waits for a shower to open. The sights and smells and sounds of evening surround her as she muses briefly on Frank and suicide, considering the good fortune of the Germans being wholly uninterested in the Rocky Mountain States. One of her students talks with her briefly, and the specter of increased occupation arises. Later, at dinner, she makes talk with a local restauranteur as truckers look on. Juliana talks with one of them, and casual racism emerges. Juliana muses on Frank again before talking with the trucker, Joe, again. Tensions emerge and a fight almost begins, but it stops before starting. Juliana asks Joe where he will be staying and makes a recommendation for a hotel. She also assesses him, setting aside the thought that he is an operative. She also muses on German inbreeding and sexual depravity – which leads to its present. Joe asks Juliana for a ride to the hotel.

As a rocket begins to descend into San Francisco, Baynes converses with a fellow passenger, stunning him with a refusal or inability to speak German. He voices his cover story of being a Swedish plastics merchant, and the two discuss the function of art as well as San Francisco. Baynes takes exception to comments from his interlocutor and muses on the German psychosis. He considers the German character and striving towards ideal forms, realizing that a mass indulgence of a single archetype has seized them. He notes his Jewishness to his interlocutor and notes that due to his own placement, he could have the interlocutor taken as a Jew. The interlocutor is shaken as Baynes departs and meets with Tagomi, who awaits him. Tagomi offers a gift, which Baynes accepts; the gift is described as Baynes and Tagomi depart together.

Chapter 4

Frank considers his former employer, who is described, as he makes to meet with him. The company's standing is noted, and Frank confronts the old employer, who passes him off to Ed. They converse briefly, and Ed notes the possibility of Frank going into business for himself, perhaps making jewelry. Frank questions the viability of such a thing, and Ed notes that some shops – such as Childan's – might carry their wares. The forged goods they also carry are noted; Frank had been one of the better forgers I his former employer's operation. The fake antiques industry is noted, along with the unthinking acceptance that supports it. Frank voices objections to the idea, which Ed allays; Frank muses on his excellence as a foreman and makes to consult the I Ching for advice on the venture. The forecast is largely favorable, although problems will soon arise for him whether he goes into business or not. He lets Ed know he will work, and Ed invites him to dinner. Frank continues to consider the bad omen he has received and muses on Juliana.

Childan, recalling the meeting with Tagomi in some detail, goes to lunch. After he returns, he is confronted by a man who presents himself as an aide to a Japanese admiral who is in search of gifts for his officers. Childan trots out materials for review, and the man condemns them as forged. Childan is taken aback as the man leaves; he had not known the materials were forged and seeks to verify authenticity. The news is not good; the materials are, indeed, forged. Childan calls his supplier and complains; he also determines that the visitor who had occasioned the revelation is himself a fraud. Childan panics somewhat about how to proceed.

Chapter 5

Frank's former employer receives a call from Childan's supplier, noting the exposure. They discuss the event, and the employer realizes that Frank and Ed are behind it. He considers how to handle the matter, partly in consultation with his mistress, and mulls over turning Frank in as a Jew. He also makes a show of demonstrating the falsity of authenticity, and the mistress leaves. As she does, she strongly suggests that he read The Grasshopper Lies Heavy, describing the text's (alternate) alternate historical scope. He rejects the suppositions as not only false, but implausibly false, and discussion of German dominion in the former eastern United States ensues. The mistress leaves.

Tagomi and Baynes take tea, discussing the value of the I Ching. Baynes is somewhat confused by the conversation, nursing a headache as he ponders his situation. They note that a third party from mainland Japan will attend their more formal meeting later. That third party, Yatabe, is described. Discussion of treatment of elders ensues, and Tagomi asks for a neutral Swedish opinion on the matter that Baynes struggles to give. The threat of German racism being turned against Japan is voiced, as well. Baynes considers that his earlier comments have occasioned the current situation, and he muses on the ability to speak openly – but he almost breaks his cover against another man speaking Swedish.

Chapter 6

In the morning, Juliana shops for groceries, mulling over her necessary errands and looking at recent news. Media depiction of Germans attracts attention, and she considers German humorlessness. She considers German politics as she continues her errands, and when she returns home, she sees Joe still in her bed. She considers him as she puts groceries away, and when she wakes him, she is taken by a strange fear. He notes that he will be picked up again later, and she considers him further, learning his age and eliciting stories of wartime activities from him. The stories include the loss of his brothers to British commandos. Joe brings out a copy of The Grasshopper Lies Heavy, asking Juliana about its contents. She notes that she has not read the book, and he remarks that the author depicts Italy turning on the Axis to secure Allied victory. Juliana considers reading the text and notes to Joe that the only text she generally carries is the I Ching, which Joe disregards. She considers him yet further as news comes that the German Chancellor has died; mourning is declared, and Juliana and Joe mull over who will succeed the deceased leader. Juliana voices revulsion at some of the prospects, and Joe remarks that only placement differentiates them before railing against the old aristocracy. Juliana asks how Joe came to have the book, and he answers. He also asks about Abdensen, who is described along with his High Castle. They argue briefly, leaving Juliana unsettled.

Tagomi takes a moment to reflect. He considers what he knows of Baynes, including his reality as a German operative. Even so, he looks forward to the formal meeting with Baynes and Yatabe. Ramsey breaks in with news about the death of the German Chancellor, and Tagomi takes stock of appropriate responses – including maintaining contact with Japan. A summons comes from the Japanese governor, which Tagomi attends in haste. He joins many there as a briefing on likely successors is conducted. Various German officials are described, generally unfavorably. Tagomi finds himself ill and leaves in haste, feeling himself shamed for doing so and struggling to recover his equanimity after the shocking revelation of actual evil. He returns to his office and arranges to be briefed on the briefing. When news comes, it confirms that the official view of German practice is that it is economically ruinous and that the ruin will likely drive recklessness from the German hierarchy. After, Tagomi dictates his message to the local German consul, doing so with difficulty. After that, Baynes calls, asking after Yatabe with some concern. Tagomi mulls over the misfortunes of the day, consulting the oracle; Ramsey asks after the static result.

Frank consults the oracle, occasioning chagrin from Ed, as blackmail money comes from their former employer. Ed purposes to use the money to outfit their business endeavor; the workspace secured already is described. Frank muses on the bad beginning of their business, Ed exhorting him to look forward.

Chapter 7

Childan is invited to the Kasouras' home. His approach thereto is described, including the questioning stares he receives from the exclusively Japanese residents of their neighborhood. The Kasouras greet him warmly, and their apartment is described as he enters it. They discuss dinner, and Childan offers his guest-gift, a bit of scrimshaw. The gift is accepted, and Childan begins to relax, reviewing his circumstances. He also muses on the peace of the Kasouras, reflecting on the philosophical underpinnings thereof. Small talk turns to developments in Germany, noting unrest and quelling actions. Childan realizes he is speaking out of turn and is shamed thereby; he considers himself likely already ruined for them and works not to show his lust for Betty. He asks after a book they appear to have been reading, The Grasshopper Lies Heavy. They discuss it, Betty arguing that it is not science fiction in a true sense – an interesting bit of metacommentary from Dick. They offer to loan him the text, which he refuses, again faltering. Talk turns to music, which is another point of gentle contention between Paul and Betty and which leaves Childan at a loss. It returns to the book briefly before dinner is served. The meal is good, leaving Childan to consider his usual meals; talk returns to the book, and Childan voices support for the current regime – to the sadness of the Kasouras. He finds himself confused, then angry at the perceived Japanese imitativeness, and he reflects on the differences. Paul attempts to engage Childan again, but Childan sidesteps it and considers further the differences between the Japanese and others.

At length, Childan heads home, reviewing the evening's events. Along the way, local police confront him, asking about the false aide (see Chapter 4, above). Childan confirms the appearance of the culprit, now identified as Frank, and signs a statement to that effect. He considers the deceit perpetrated upon him and muses anti-Semitically. He also purposes to buy a copy of The Grasshopper Lies Heavy, thinking to find out what is special about the text, and he longs to live under German rule.

Chapter 8

Reiss arrives at his office and receives a coded message and a request to return a call to the head of secret police in the area. Reiss reads the news, learning about developments in the succession to the Chancellorship, and muses on his relationship with the police head. Said head calls again, asking for updates on an intelligence agent. Reiss reports that the agent has not reported to him and realizes that the agent has eluded control. The police head notes that the agent, Wegener, is to be taken. Reiss receives a report that a Jew has been seen in the city and discusses upcoming leadership changes with his staff. The coded message is finally delivered, noting that Tedeki is inbound. Implications thereof are considered. Complications of timing are addressed, and Reiss muses acidly on other races. He then tries to read The Grasshopper Lies Heavy despite repeated interruptions and the illegality of his doing so. Another coded message comes in, noting that Goebbels has given a rousing speech that is to be reproduced and distributed. Reiss muses on the failure to get the Japanese to suppress the text and on Abdensen's authorial ability, as well as the danger of his book. He considers having Abdensen killed and rages at the circumstances in which he finds himself as he makes to read Goebbles's speech.

Chapter 9

After two weeks, Frank and Ed have a full batch of jewelry ready and business cards to match. Their work is described, as is their work setup. Ed goes to make a sales pitch to Childan, going since Frank cannot – although Frank will do most of the rest of the selling. Frank considers fallback options and muses on what the oracle has said. He thinks on how Juliana would succeed in selling the jewelry without trouble, and he considers sending her a piece of his work. Juilana's need for company comes to his mind, and Ed makes to push their wares on Childan. He smokes a marijuana cigarette to calm himself as Frank continues to muse on Juliana's life and need for company, thinking himself too rough for her; Ed approves his sending pieces to her. Frank continues to consider as Ed moves off.

After sex, Juliana holds Joe. She muses on the end of their assignation wistfully, and Joe comments on her downcast demeanor. He suggests that they go to Denver together, take a nice trip; he has the money to fund it. She notices a peculiar pen and asks about it; he handles it gingerly, and Joe presses upon her, speaking strangely. She notes his ability to arm himself adroitly as he waxes eloquent about his fighting experience. Juliana considers that he might well be lying, but sets aside fears against what seems an obvious ploy. He reads again from The Grasshopper Lies Heavy, occasioning comment.

Childan receives Ed with some disdain, viewing him sourly as he muses over recent events and the falsity of authenticity. Childan stumbles onto the idea of Ed as an amateur and works to take advantage of him, exploiting his naïveté to secure an arrangement greatly in Childan's favor as he attends to occasional customers. Childan selects piece for his own use as he does so, writing out a receipt even as he plans to defraud Ed. After the latter leaves, Childan considers the pieces and how he will profit from them. He also stumbles on the idea of making a subtle gift to Betty.

Frank is not pleased when Ed returns and reports that Childan has taken many pieces on consignment. Ed pleads enthusiasm.

Chapter 10

Baynes waits for two weeks to meet with Yatabe. He is frustrated at the delay and the stalling tactics Tagomi uses. He muses on the oddity of being able to travel quickly, only to have to wait. News arrives that Goebbels has succeeded to the German Chancellorship, and Baynes calls Tagomi. Tagomi takes the call, noting that Yatabe has not arrived. Baynes reflects on his mission, making contact with the Japanese military's representative before returning to Berlin – now changed by the succession. He considers meeting with the local German secret police chief and muses on the possibility of discovery or of already having been discovered. Leaving information with Tagomi suggests itself, but the idea is soon discarded. He goes out to clear his head and make contact with intelligence resources. Doing so comforts him.

Juliana and Joe drive for Denver, discussing music along the way. Joe rails about German control of artistic production as Juliana reads from The Grasshopper Lies Heavy, reviewing more of Abdensen's work. Joe muses on the incorporation of the good of the occupation into the work, and Juliana continues reading. Juliana asks about the ending, which Joe reports; Britain ascends, and the United States degenerates – in large part because of its political traditions. Joe continues, decrying Anglo-Saxon plutarchy and exalting Italian fascist doctrine. Joe broaches the idea of meeting Abdensen, an idea Juliana approves heartily. They make plans to do so.

The next morning sees Tagomi consult the oracle. Omens are mixed; something major is coming. It unsettles him greatly. Yatabe calls, and they arrange to meet with Baynes. He informs Baynes and makes ready.

Baynes muses on the news and makes ready. He exults in the impending completion of his work.

Chapter 11

Reiss arrives at his office to find the police head waiting for him. Wegener has been found, his cover as Baynes identified. Quiet motion is to be made to return him to Germany, the difficulty with which Reiss notes. Plans to act against Wegener are made and confirmed by a call from Goebbels. Reiss follows orders, authorizing action with little pleasure. Potential fallout from both success and failure is noted, and Reiss considers how he might interdict the police head. Reiss resumes business.

Childan makes to meet with Paul. He is received quickly and tries to explain himself; Paul notes that the gift intended for Betty did not reach her. Paul notes having discussed it with colleagues; after initial repudiation of the piece, they agree that it has a strangely artistic value. Paul waxes eloquent on the artistic value, in fact, and returns the piece to Childan, who is confused by the gesture. Paul presses on, convincing Childan to make tchotchkes of the artwork and thus to quash the possibility of American artwork as respectable. Childan rejects the course of action and receives an apology, in which he takes quiet delight.

Chapter 12

Ramsey introduces Yatabe to Tagomi, and Tagomi recognizes Yatabe's true identity. Baynes is late, for which Tagomi apologizes. After Ramsey excuses himself, Tagomi reports to Tedeki. Tedeki notes the likelihood that Baynes is surveilled. He arrives and is admitted; he drops his persona and reports a project Dandelion, one that will facilitate the destruction of the Japanese mainland. Some information will have changed due to the succession – but Goebbles is in favor of carrying out the operation. Wegener requests Japanese intervention in the succession, undermining the stability that would allow Goebbels to act against Japan in such a way. Tagomi is struck by the moral dilemmas involved. How to proceed is discussed, with likely intermediaries named. Wegener provides Tedeki with documentation supporting his accounts. German forces breach the building in search of Wegener; Tagomi arms himself, and they wait for the assault.

Frank and Ed continue to make jewelry, Frank considering the failure of their business. He voices his concerns to Ed and asks to be bought out. Ed refuses, pending more work to sell their materials. Frank senses impending defeat as he goes outside to smoke. As he does, he is arrested and taken into custody for his shenanigans with Childan. His Jewishness is revealed, and he is told he will be remanded to German custody.

As they wait, Tedeki, Wegener and Tagomi attempt to secure assistance against the assault. Tedeki plies Japanese military contacts. Tagomi calls Reiss, to no avail. He then calls the police head and rants about the assault. The attack reaches Tagomi's office, and Tagomi kills the intruders – to his own detriment. The others take the weapons of the slain, and political fallout is discussed. Tagomi tries to consult the oracle about events, and Tedeki notes to Wegener that Tagomi is reacting badly to having killed people. Complications associated therewith are explicated.

Chapter 13

Juliana and Joe go shopping in Denver. Her new clothes are detailed, and Joe issues surprising edicts for how she should dress when meeting Abdensen. Joe gets his hair cut and dyed, and Juliana sees to his new outfitting and exults in the possibilities of their situation as they check in to their hotel; it is described. There, they buy a copy of The Grasshopper Lies Heavy, and Joe asserts that they will press on that evening. Juliana balks, but Joe presses on and makes to get ready for dinner. Juliana balks further, taken aback by his sudden haste. Her thought turn to Frank, and Joe threatens to kill her. She responds with threats of her own and questions Joe; he reveals himself as an intelligence operative sent to assassinate Abdensen. Juliana speaks of Seattle as she suffers an anxiety attack; Joe drugs her against it. She staggers to and through the bathroom, arming herself, and she slits his throat. She slowly collects herself and flees, considering what she should do as she finds a place to park and consults the oracle. The omen suggests that she press on to meet Abdensen and reveals that other assassins will move against him. She drives thence to Cheyenne, where Abdensen lives, and calls his house; arrangements are made for her to call on the house the next day. After, she eats and finds a motel.

Chapter 14

Tagomi wanders about the city, contemplating what he must do and the information he has gained through the meeting and his own actions. He calls on Childan's shop, trying to rid himself of the gun he had used to kill the assailants (see Chapter 12, above); Childan refuses to take the merchandise back, but he presses some of Ed and Frank's work on Tagomi, suggesting that they can work upon him in time. Tagomi accepts a piece and wanders on. At a park, he contemplates the piece given him, finding chastisement from it and no ease of his inner turmoil; he continues to consider the piece, testing methodically with his senses and stumbling into its artistic effect. A passing policeman breaks his reverie, and Tagomi considers urban blight. He continues to seek solace, failing to find it. At length, he makes his way to work.

At his office, Ramsey expresses concern for him and reports that the mess from the assault has been cleaned. Tedeki is back en route to Japan, and Wegener has departed. Reiss arrives, and their meeting is tense. Tagomi notes having killed two, and Reiss disavows them. Tagomi then upbraids Germany through Reiss and orders Frank's release as a way to spite the German consul. As Reiss leaves, Tagomi suffers a heart attack and is tended to as he muses over what is to come.

Frank is released form police custody. He muses on his strange good fortune and makes to return to work with Ed.

Chapter 15

Wegener returns to Germany, musing on what will happen next, both for the world and for himself. He is greeted on his return by uniformed personnel who tell him he will be taken to a particular officer; it brings him some small hope, but only a small hope against the insanity he knows is endemic to the German government. The path taken kills his small hope, and he muses on the folly of it all.

Juliana makes for the Abdensen residence, noting news of her actions in Denver the night before; she is not known as the culprit responsible for Joe's death. She arranges for a room and reads Abdensen's book fully. After a dinner, she makes to dress for her meeting and considers calling Frank; he does not answer, and Juliana presses on.

The Abdensen house is described as Juliana approaches it. She is welcomed in and introduced; Abdensen himself is described. His current living situation is explicated. Juliana asks after his use of I Ching, which he denies. He is slow in answering her, and she warns him of coming assassination attempts. Abdensen's use of the oracle to forecast his success is noted, and he presses on

Juliana to make a prediction. She does so and finds that Abdensen's book is true, despite the observable reality in which they exist. The implications are not explciated, and Juliana departs.

ANALYSIS OF A KEY CHARACTER

The Man in the High Castle prominently features Frank "Frink" Fink. Appropriately named, he is a shifty character, working as a forger and impersonating a military officer as he – admittedly understandably, given the circumstances – hides his identity. Much of the action of the text follows his exploits, and he serves as the unifying character of the novel; it is only through association with him that the various strands of the plot interconnect (see "Plot Analysis," above). He serves therefore as something of a primary protagonist, although he is an odd sort of one, being in many ways antithetical to many of the traditions at work in the genre.

MAJOR SYMBOLS

No small number of symbols pervade the text, many of which are explicated at great length in scholarly papers. One that attracts attention is marigolds, which appear in floral arrangements throughout the novel. They are a thoroughly domestic, homely flower, useful in the preparation of food and for some degree of bug repelling. It also can be used medicinally and in the preparation of yellow dye – and there is some association of those who cultivate the flowers with aspiration to navigate the Japanese – derisively "yellow" – society imposed upon what had been the western United States.

A more important symbol is the in-milieu novel, The Grasshopper Lies Heavy. Titled after Ecclesiastes 12:5, the book is itself an alternate history from the alternate history – not a vision of the "real" world, but of a different world in which the English-speaking powers won the Second World War and the British Empire returned to dominance of the world. Given the association of Ecclesiastes with timeliness – Ecclesiastes 3 famously opens "To every thing there is a season, and a time to every purpose under the heaven" – and of Dick with prophetic, ecstatic visions, it can be read as a portent of things to come. It can also be read as a commendation of the state of affairs in the real world when Dick wrote, one that acknowledges that things are better than they well could have been.

MOTIFS

A recurring pattern in *The Man in the High Castle* is reference to works of literature as guideposts for the text. Both the real I Ching and the in-milieu The Grasshopper Lies Heavy (see "Major Symbols" above) appear repeatedly in the work, used by various characters as methods for ascertaining what to do next, how to proceed and how to interpret the events that befall them. Some such use is to be expected; any author can be assumed to value text, and encouraging recourse to texts serves writers well. That the texts in question are an oracle and a work of fiction, however, suggests that readers can find value in the discussion of what might be as much as what is – something particularly relevant for those who will write works of speculative fiction.

THEMES

Several themes emerge from the text. One is particularly relevant to the time of the novel's initial publication: racism. The major Axis powers, Germany and Japan, were both noted historically for their xenophobic attitudes; the Holocaust and the Japanese ill-regard for those other than Yamato Japanese are both amply attested. The continuation of such attitudes in what had been the United States is noted, and there are no few references to racial and ethnic epithets and distinctions of caste based upon ethnicity and race in the text. The early 1960s in the real world saw much done to advance causes of civil rights – although the work continues decades later – so the association of racism with a dystopian future serves as a commentary on the state of affairs current with the novel's publication.

Another is relevant to the genre in which the novel exists and more generally to the United States as a whole. In the text, there is a privileging of older works of art in the United States; the old and antique are particularly valuable for reasons that are never made completely clear. Concomitantly, the new is rejected throughout most of the text. A similar situation obtains for the United States, which suffers some dislocation due to its relatively short history, as well as to speculative fiction, which suffers under an onus of juvenility. Dick and other writers in the genre, despite being remarkably skilled wordsmiths and anticipating technological and social developments that have come to pass, worked against the prevailing assumption that they treated the unreal because they could not handle the real; their work was a new thing, one still regarded uneasily despite its potential, sometimes realized, for quality.

CONCLUSION

The Man in the High Castle offers readers a chilling glimpse of an alternate history, one in which the facts upon which the later twentieth century are fiction only. Unlike many dystopian works, it does not portray a uniformly negative view of the way things might have fallen out; there is good, admittedly less among the successors of Hitler than among those of Tojo, but there was and remains much ill among those who won the Second World War in the real world. In the novel, Dick holds up something of a mirror to those ills; perhaps hope remains to correct some of them.

THOUGHT PROVOKING /OR DISCUSSION QUESTIONS

To help guide further consideration of the text, the following questions might be useful. Answers to each can do much to help readers get more from the reading they do. Also a fantastic addition to anyone looking for ideas to share in their book club.

Author

- Does the author use his/her real name or a pseudonym? If the latter, what kind of person is implied by the pseudonym?

- What else has the author written? How does this book compare to the other things the author has written? Is it in the same genre?

- Is this book in a series the author writes? If so, where does it fit in the series?

Plot

- Is the plot a single, large piece?

- Is it made of several threads that move together? What unites the threads?

- Is it instead a series of short, less-connected pieces? What unites them?

- Does the plot start at the beginning of the action and move forward? Does it start in the middle and move back and forth from it? Does it follow another order entirely?

- What is the central conflict of the book? What drives it? What reasons do those on different sides of it have for their actions?

- Is the conflict person versus person, person versus nature, person versus society, person versus outside force or deity, person versus self or some other conflict?

Character

- Who is the narrator? Is it a first-person or third-person perspective? Is it limited or omniscient? What background and position does the narrator take? Is the narrator trustworthy?

- Who is the primary protagonist? What physical and psychological traits does the protagonist have?

- Who are major secondary protagonists? How do they relate to the primary protagonist? What physical and psychological traits do they have? How do they contribute to or take away from the primary protagonist?

- Who is the primary antagonist (If any)? What physical and psychological traits does the antagonist have? How does s/he oppose the protagonist?

- Who are major secondary antagonists? How do they relate to the primary antagonist? What physical and psychological traits do they have? How do they contribute to or take away from the primary antagonist? How do they oppose the protagonist?

Symbol and Motif

- When and where is the book set, or when and where is like the book is set? What associations attach to that time and place? What historical and literary events does the setting bring to mind? What associates with them?

- What colors are described most often? With what are they associated in the book? With what are they associated for you?

- Do the characters quote other books or works? What works? What lines do they quote? What associates with those quotations?

- What recurring patterns are in the text? Where do they appear: in narration, in character action, in character speech? How exactly do they repeat? How often do they repeat? With what do they associate?

Theme

- What messages does the book seem to send? How does it seem to send them?

- What social issues does the book seem to engage? How does it engage them? Are they relevant to you? Are they likely to be relevant to other readers?

Experience/Perspective/Response

- Did you feel drawn into the book immediately, or did it take time for you to get into the book? What in the book made you feel that way?

- Does anything in the book remind you of your own lived experience? What and how does it?

- How did the book make you feel overall? Satisfied? Confused? Angry? Happy? Content? Disturbed? • What in the book made you feel that way?

Ending

Did you find the ending satisfying?

- Would you change the ending? How?
- What would be the next chapter? Why?

Made in the USA
San Bernardino, CA
03 January 2016